Classroom Clips

DISPLAYS, AWARDS, & BORDERS

by Marilynn G. Barr

Publisher: Roberta Suid
Editor: Carol Whiteley

Printed in the United States of America
9 8 7 6 5 4 3 2 1

Table of Contents

INTRODUCTION

How to Use the Card Sets and Patterns

Characters Use these creatures as bulletin board display characters or stick puppets. You can also reproduce them to make into flannel board puppets, to decorate and use as cards, and use with art activities.

Borders The children can color border patterns and link them in chains to decorate the classroom. Borders can be used to frame paper crafts and/or art activities.

Corner Stones Use these patterns on bulletin board corners and to cover short border strips. They can also be glued to folders containing appropriate subject materials, worksheets, lists, etc.

Posters/Charts As classroom helper and achiever charts, these pages are great. Use them to post the children's names, to write thank you notes and notes about field trips to parents, for class parties or special events, or laminated as number of the day, letter of the day, word of the day, or king or queen for the day posters.

File Folder Patterns These can be glued to the front of file folders and attached to the bulletin board to display and/or group student work. They can also be cut out and stapled to the bulletin board for use in sorting and for worksheet storage. The pockets can be used as props and/or report covers.

Worksheet Display Awards Use these awards when you display good work papers on the bulletin board. Or white out the message and let the students use the award to make a giant greeting card.

Staple Corners These awards are ideal for grouping student work for Open House. When taped to a paper strip they make great bookmarks.

Clothespin Awards After gluing each to a clothespin, you can use the clothespins to group good student work together. You may also want to use the awards for motivation: students attach an award to the back of their chair when they have done a good job. Use the open award to flag important areas of the classroom, for bonus credit activity, or attach to furniture and/or books (use just the bumblebee) to point out the location of clues in Hide and Go Seek-type activities.

Full-Page Awards
These special awards will provide classroom or take-home recognition of achievement.

Attendance Tags After each child has colored a tag, the tags can be enlarged and posted along the bottom edge of a bulletin board, flannel board, or wall. Using pushpins or cup hooks, the students can hang their tags for an easy-to-see attendance chart or to identify classroom helpers, the student of the week, and so on.

Birthday Patterns A special badge, desk label, and frame add extra recognition on birthdays.

Props The variety of hat and play patterns are excellent for role-playing, sorting, and grouping activities. For example, you can write long vowels and short vowels on jelly bean-shaped cards and have children place either all the long vowel or all the short vowel words inside the jar.

Shape Books These are great for writing practice, for working daily math problems, to write poems, or to make into giant greeting cards (eliminate the lines if you wish). They also work well for diaries, homework notebooks, reference books for rules (math, spelling, etc), invitations to parents or other classes, and for thank you notes to class volunteers and special guests.

Doorknob Hanger The children can decorate these with art from books or with yarn, buttons, sequins, colored tissue paper, colored cellophane, and so on. The hangers make great gifts for moms, dads, and grandparents.

Clips Collections Here is a wonderful reference library of illustrations you can duplicate or enlarge for classroom displays, decorative art on worksheets, and to turn into gifts.

Teacher Notes These seasonal stationery-size notes will fit in a standard letter size envelope. Use them to write notes to students, parents, class volunteers, and lists. Duplicate the notes for students to glue on the inside of decorated construction paper greeting cards or thank you cards to class volunteers.

Bonus Business Cards Great idea! Children enjoy carrying business cards in their pockets, book bags, and wallets. These business cards entitle children to special privileges during the school year. Duplicate, color and laminate the cards for repeated use. Write the student's name on the blank with a permanent marker and when the cards are redeemed, a quick spray of hair spray and a tissue erases the name for reuse.

Craft and Gift Ideas

This section provides you with directions and diagrams for six different projects:

Greeting Cards

The children can decorate these with characters, headband strips, and card sets.

Picture Frames

Use the Birthday Frame pattern and have the children decorate their frames with craft supplies.

Doorknob Hangers

Let students decorate these with card sets and a variety of craft materials.

Refrigerator Magnets

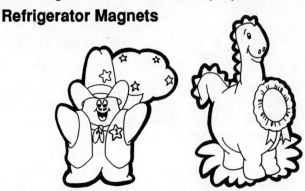

Using the Clothespin Awards (eliminate the words first) and magnetic tape, children can either mount the patterns on clothespins or laminate them and mount the magnetic tape directly on the back. (For durability, have children mount the magnetic tape prior to laminating).

Bookmarks

Children can glue art from the clothespin award patterns or borders to one end of a 1" x 6" strip of colored construction paper, then laminate.

Gift Notepads

Provide each child with construction paper covers to decorate and color. Staple 8 sheets of one or 2 sheets of each teacher note to create a Mother's Day or Grandparents' Day gift.

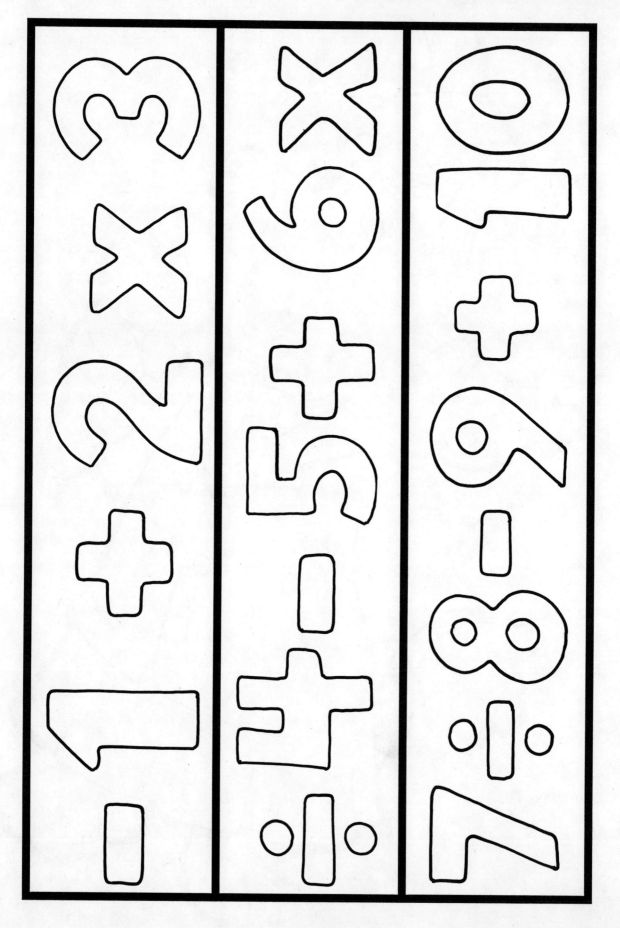

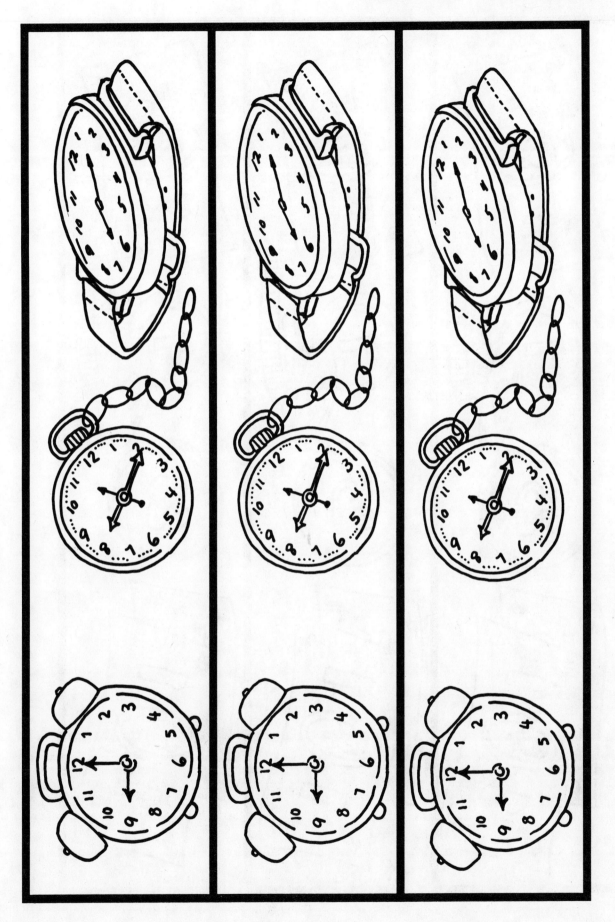

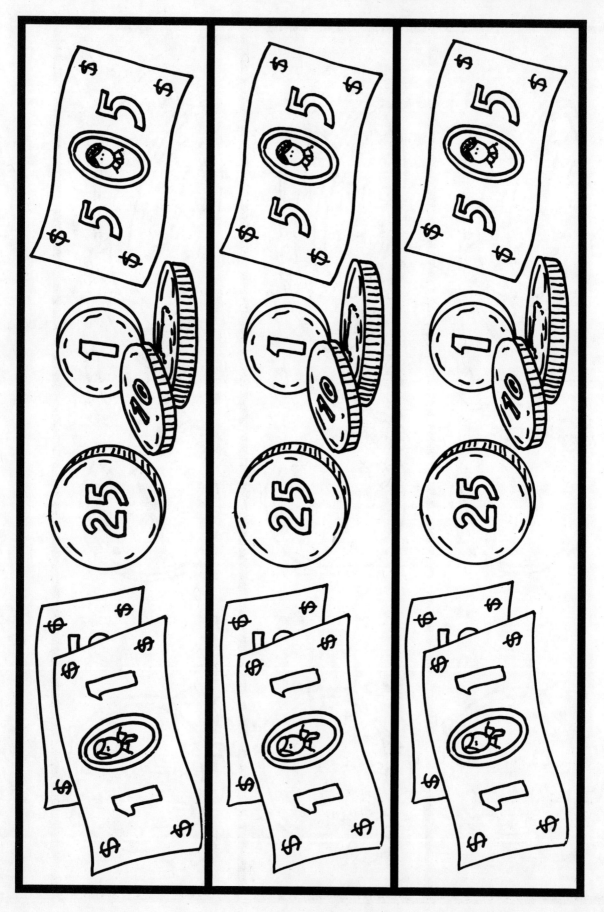

14

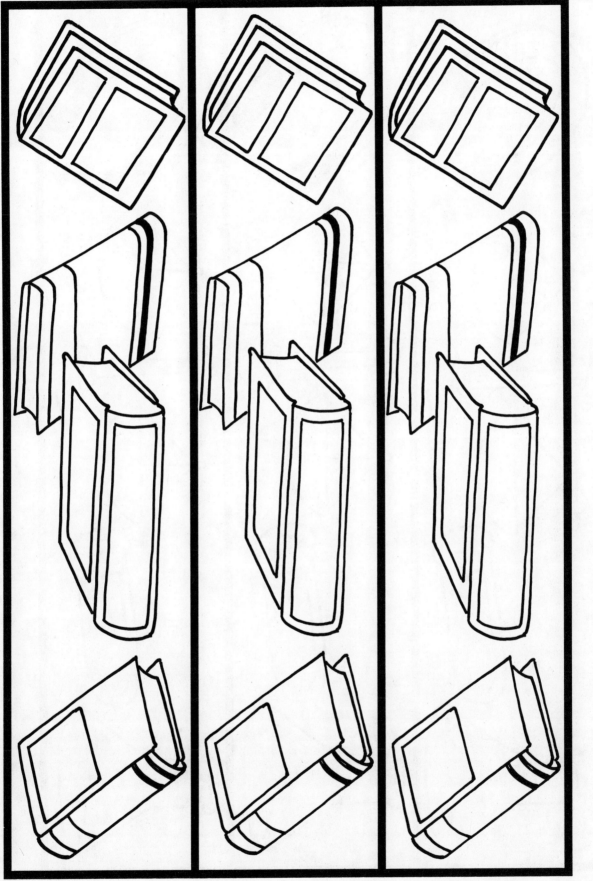

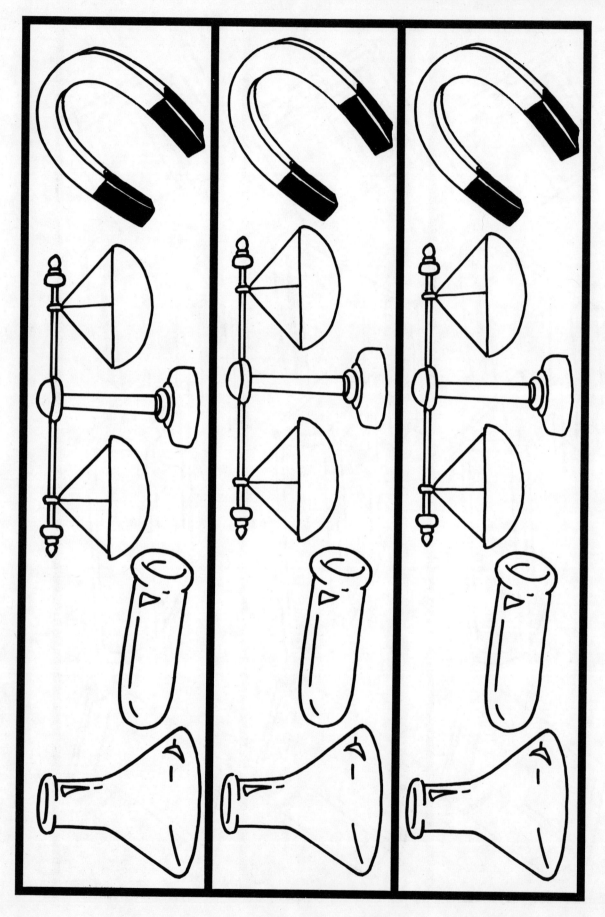

18

Bulletin Board Border

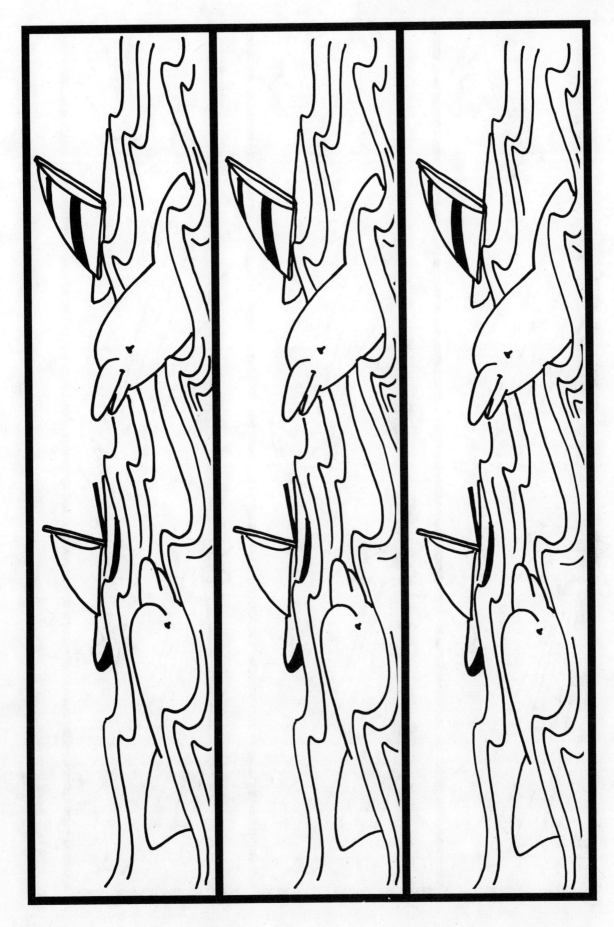

Self-
Awareness

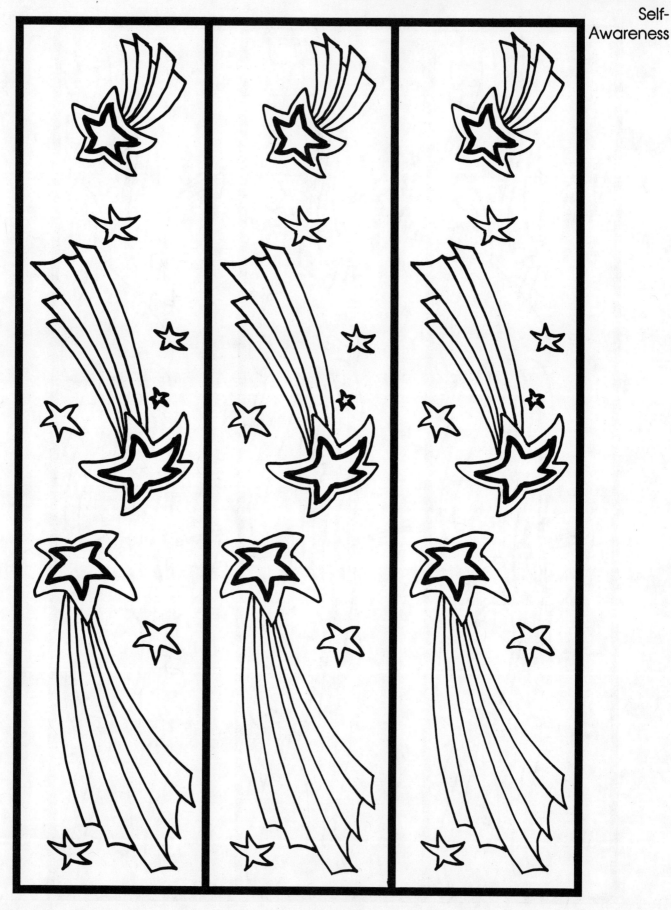

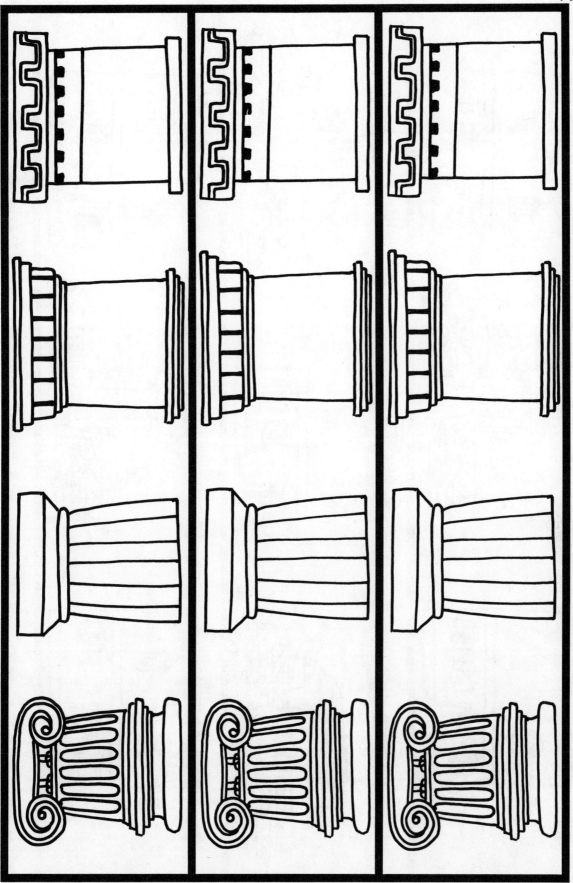

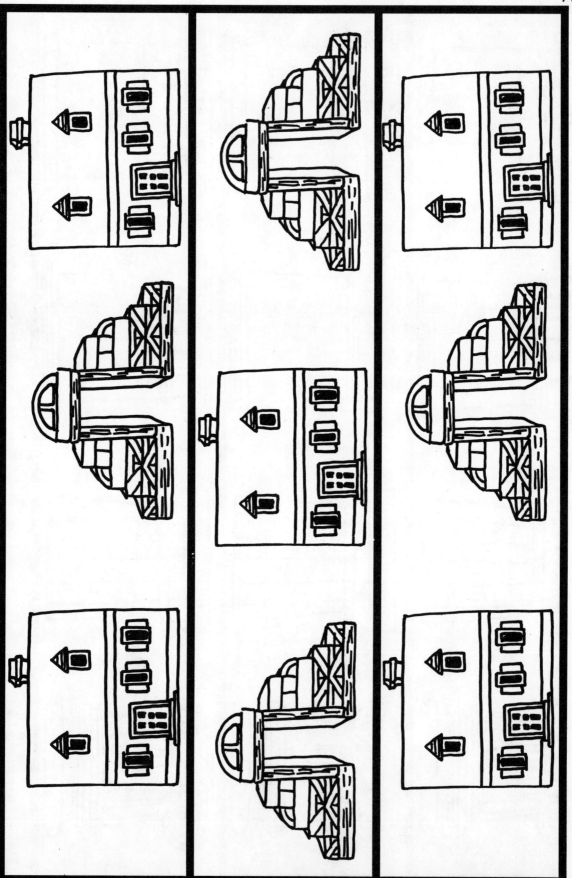

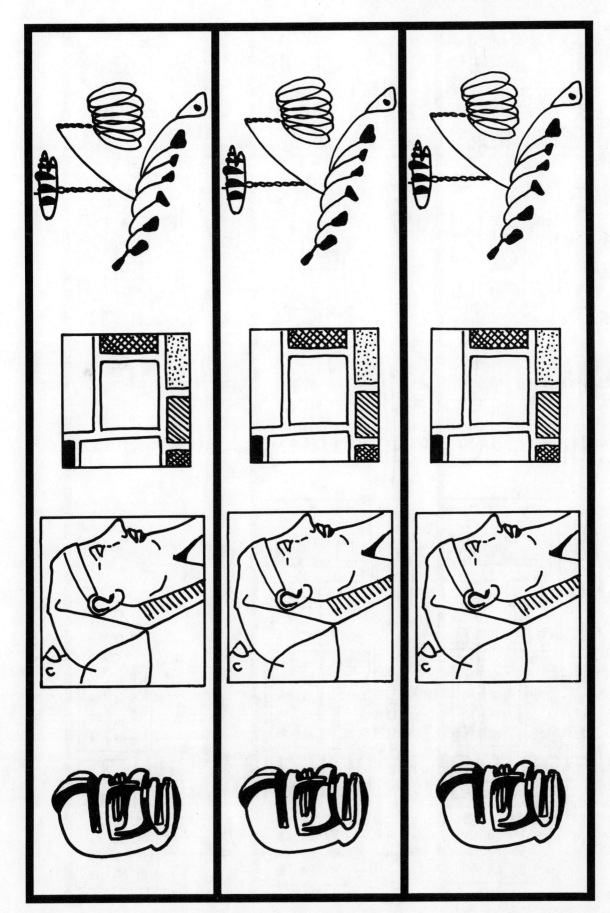

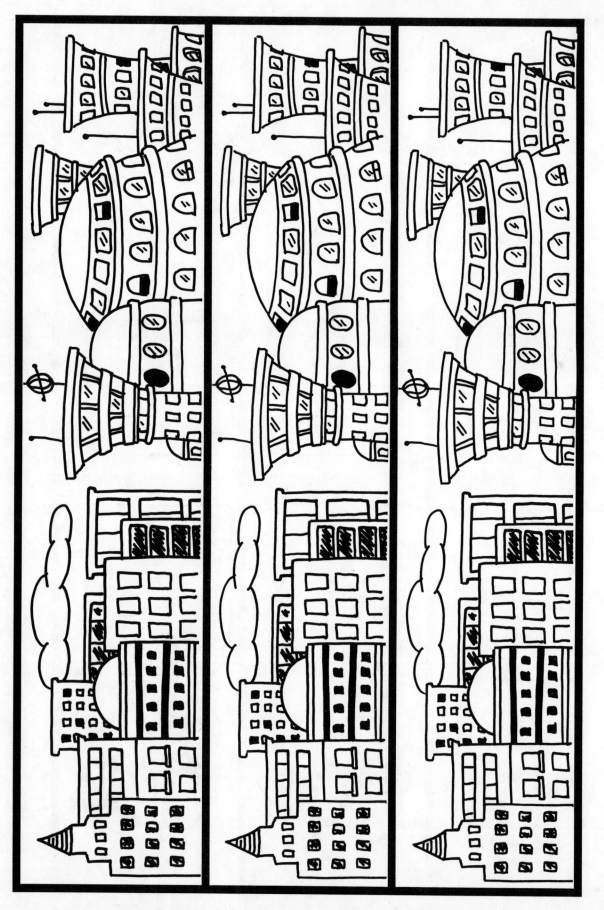

Money

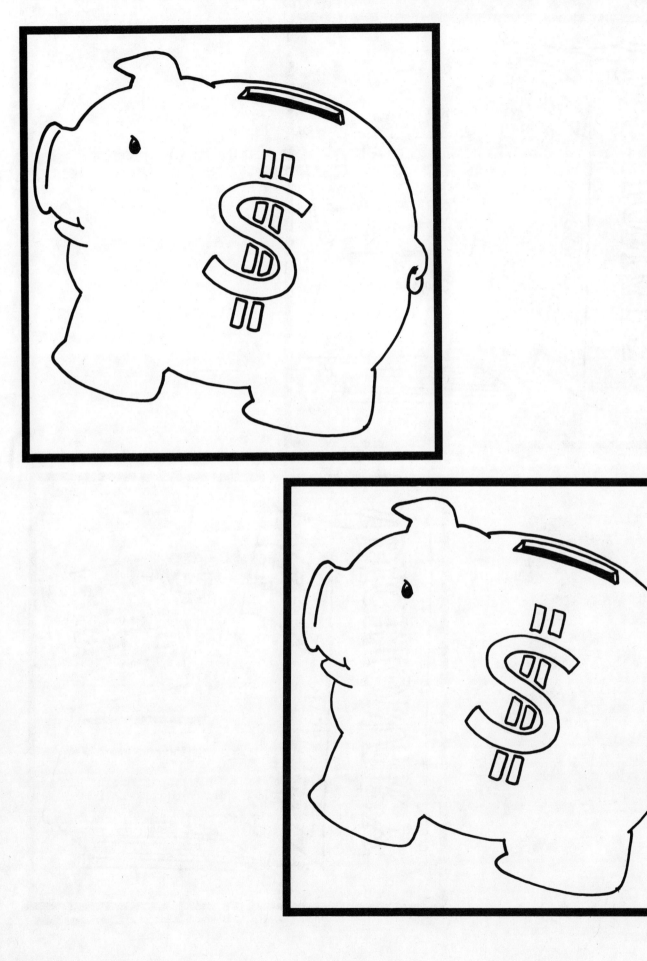

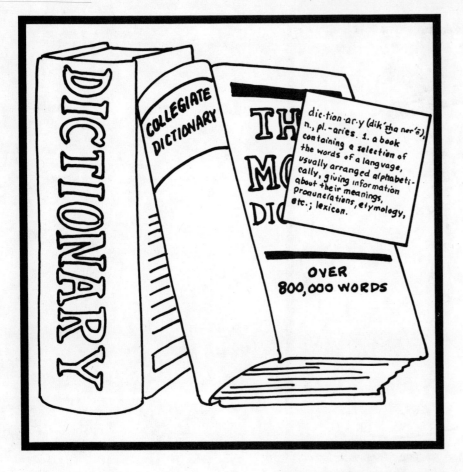

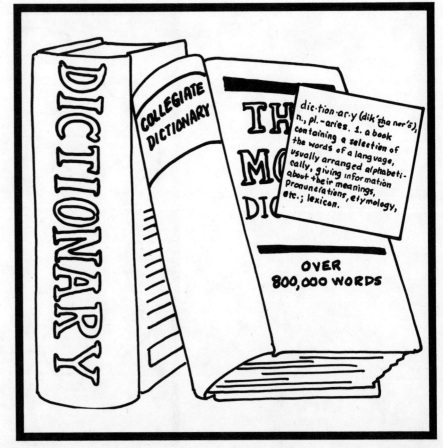

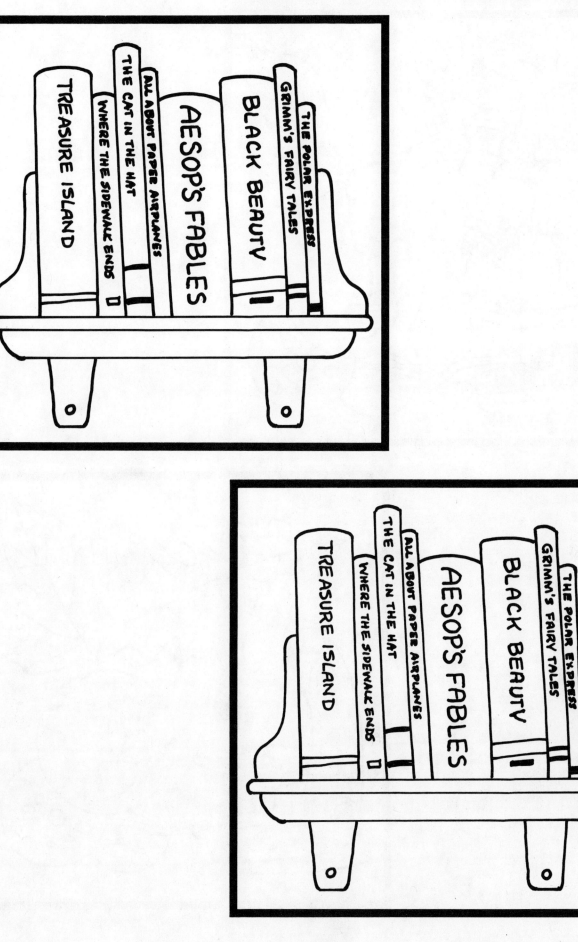

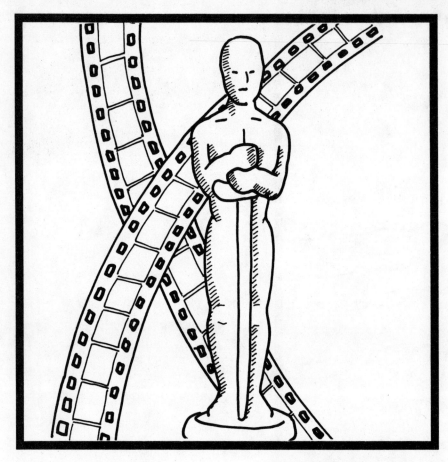

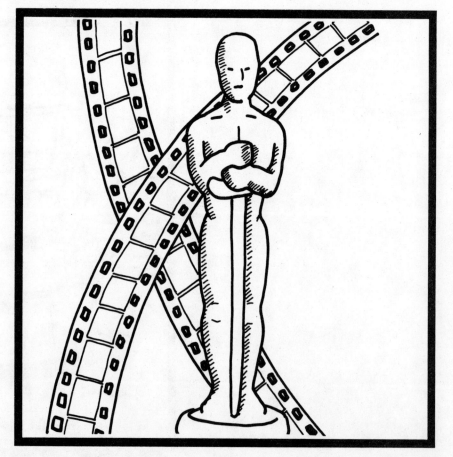

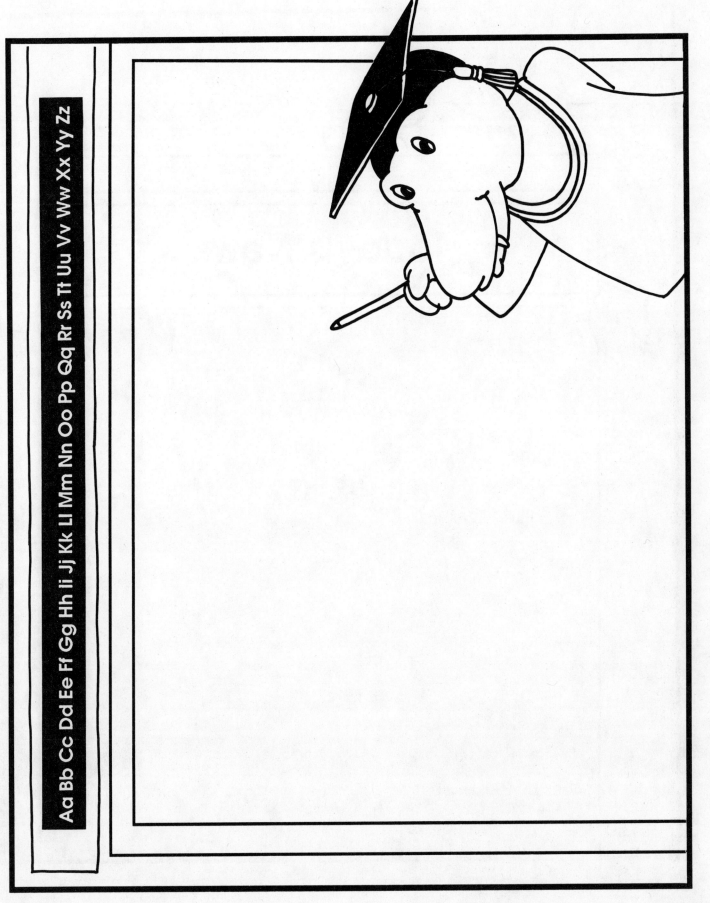

Aa Bb Cc Dd Ee Ff Gg Hh Ii Jj Kk Ll Mm Nn Oo Pp Qq Rr Ss Tt Uu Vv Ww Xx Yy Zz

Today's News

Math Folder Pattern

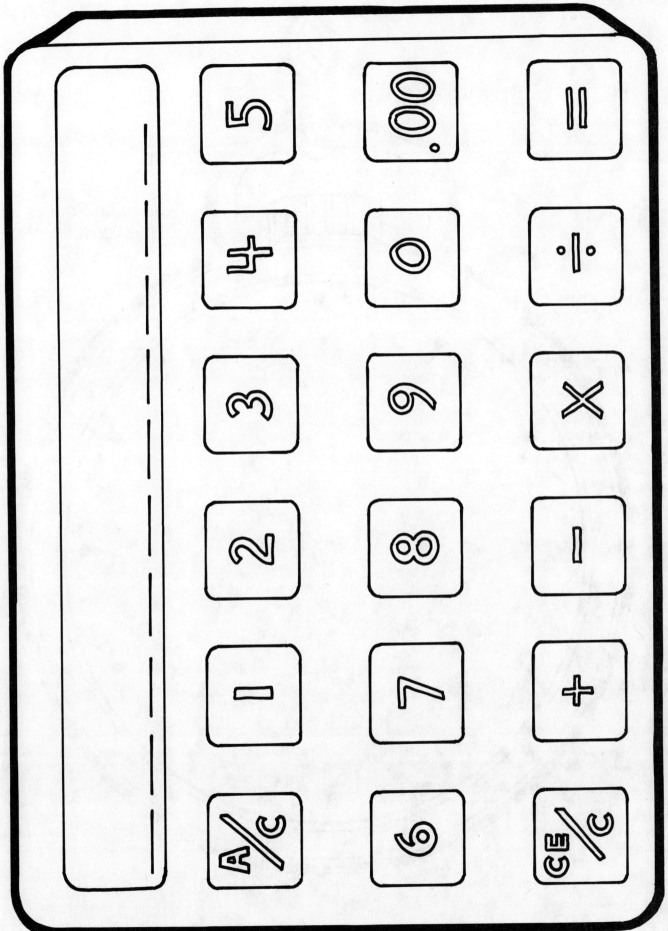

Use with *Pocket*
Time Folder Pattern.

Time Folder Pattern
Pocket

Use with *Pocket Watch*
Time Folder Pattern.

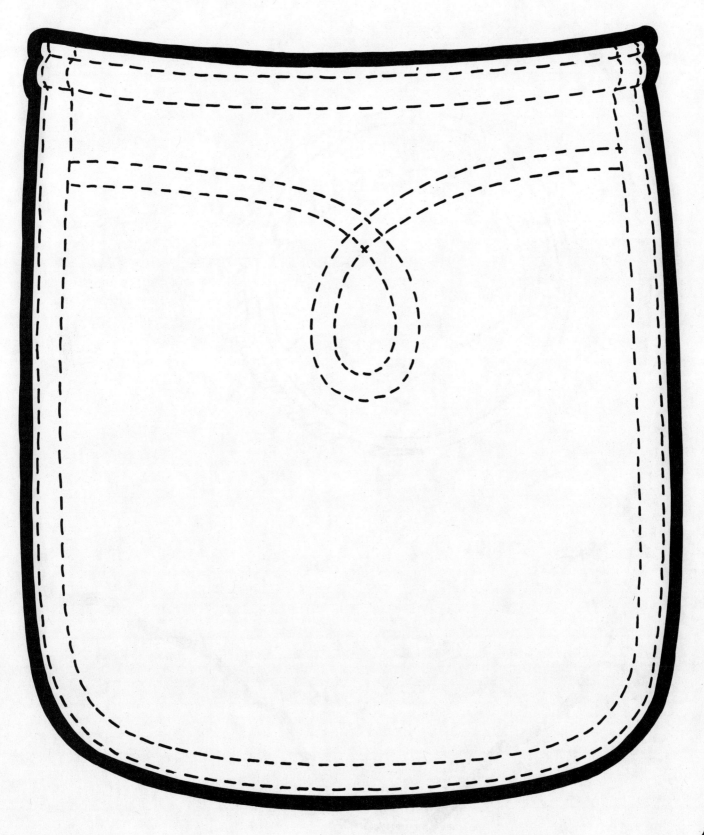

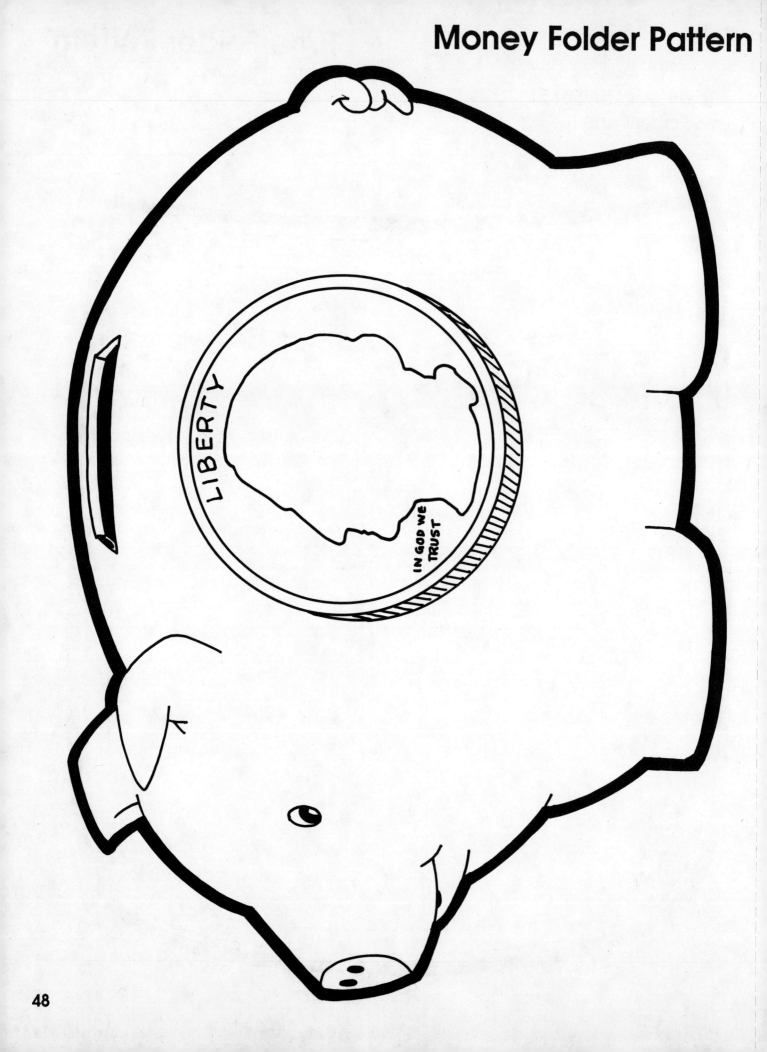

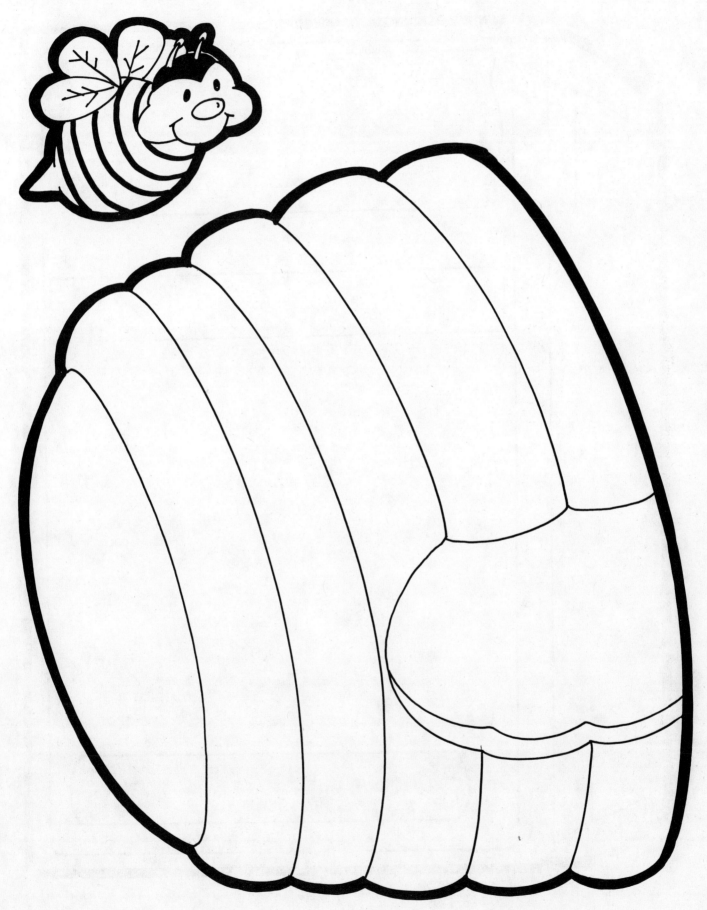

Use with *Book Jacket*
Reading Folder Pattern.

Reading Folder Pattern
A Very Special Book

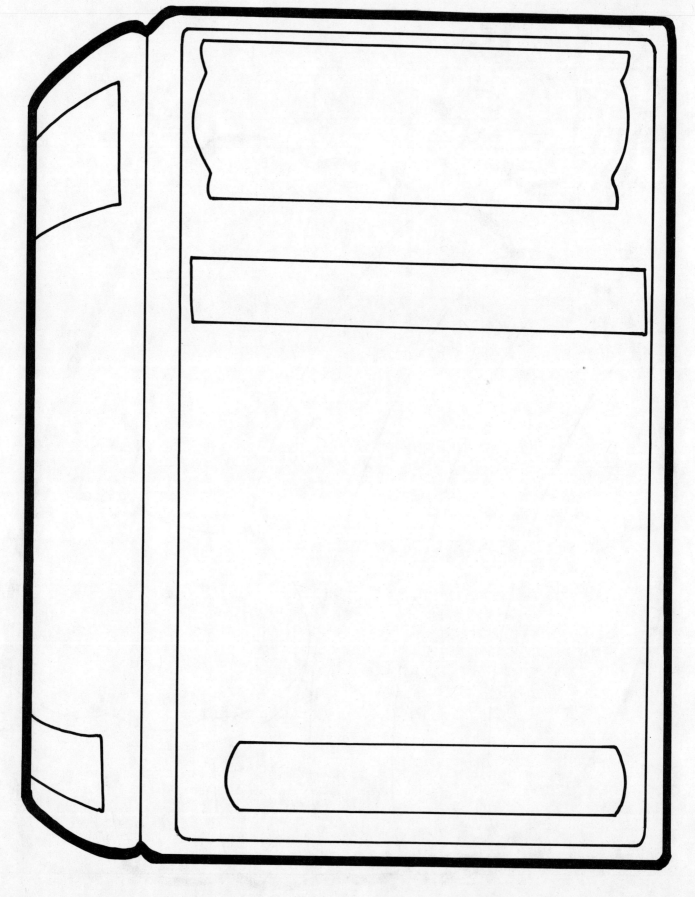

A VERY
SPECIAL BOOK

SLIT HERE BEFORE MOUNTING ON FILE FOLDER

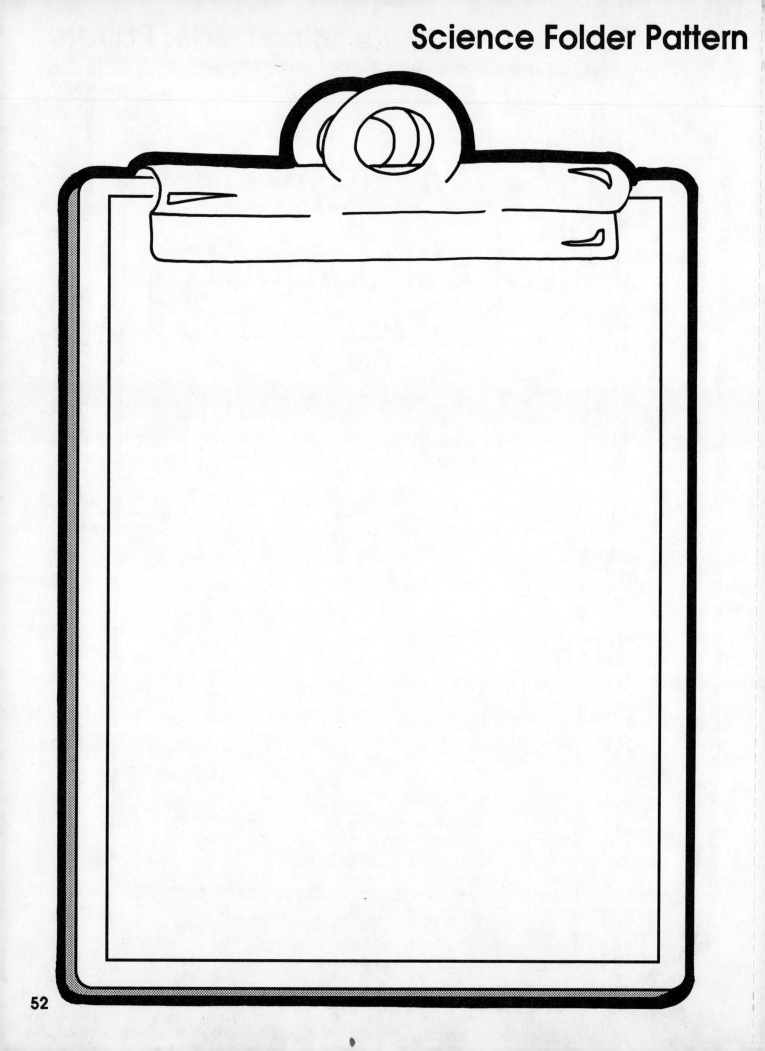

Magnificent Math!

Time Travelers - CLUB -

DAY   DATE   YEAR

Banker of the Year

Star Speller

Worksheet Display Award

Really Good Work!

ASTRO AWARD

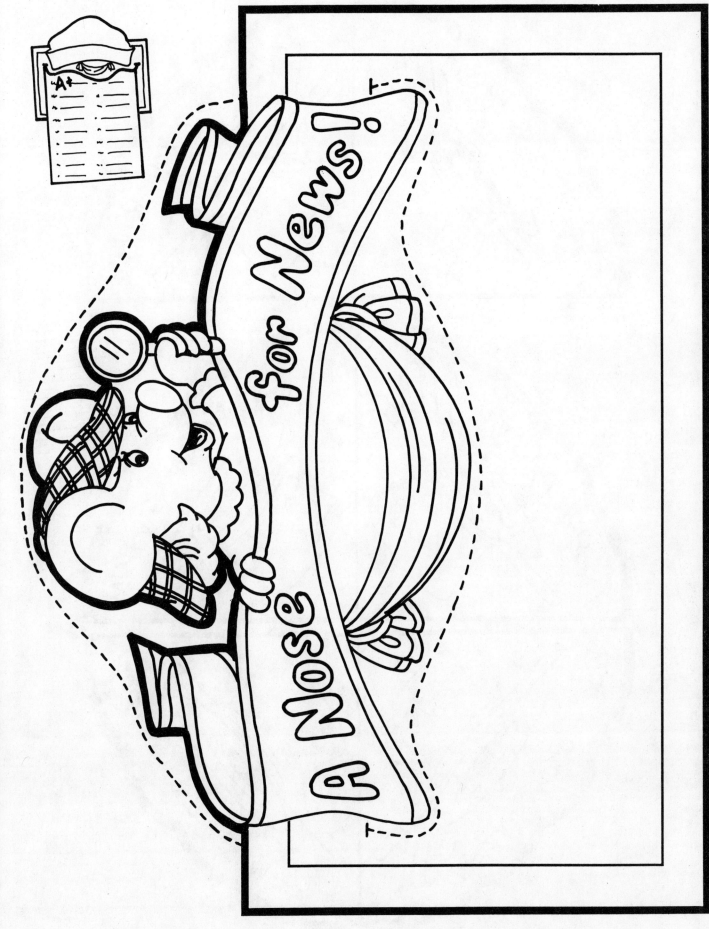

A Nose for News!

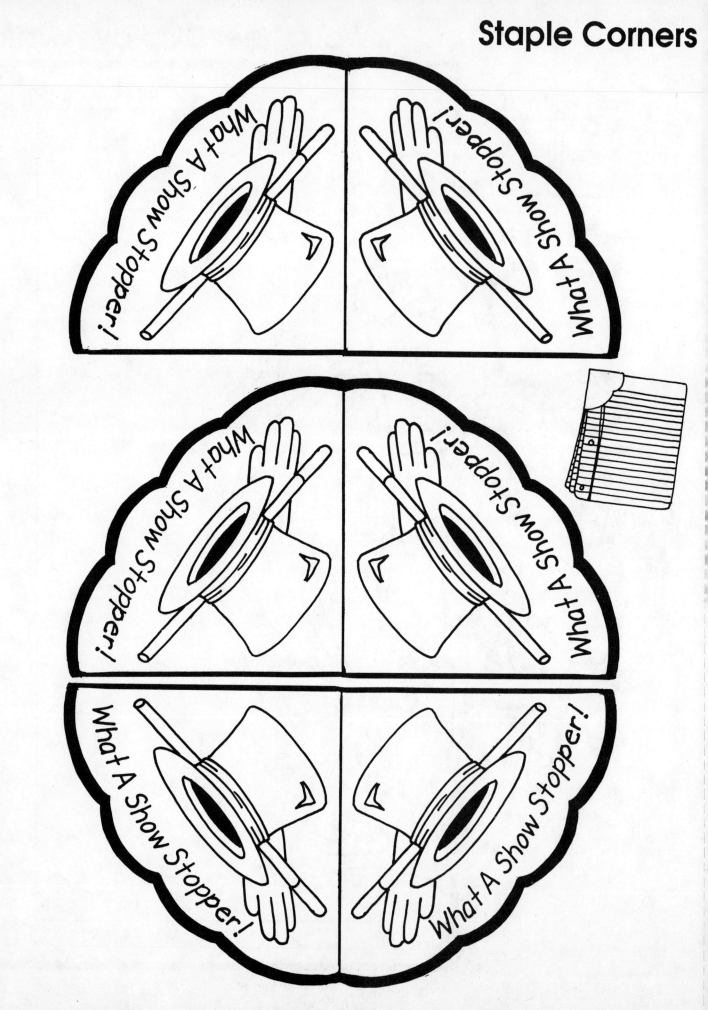

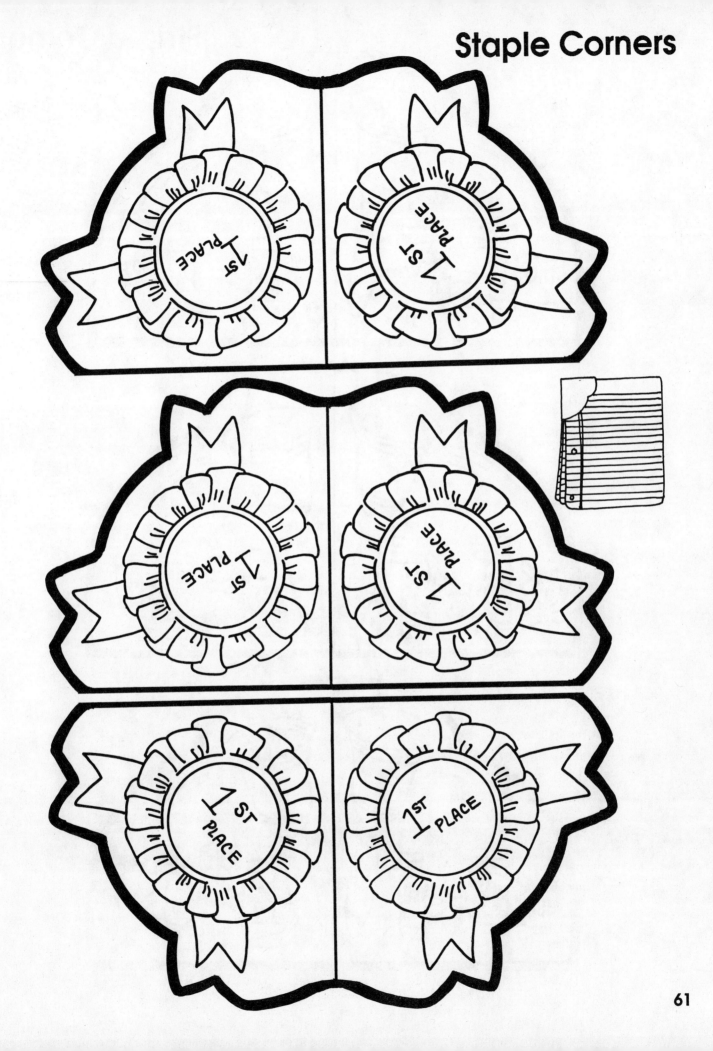

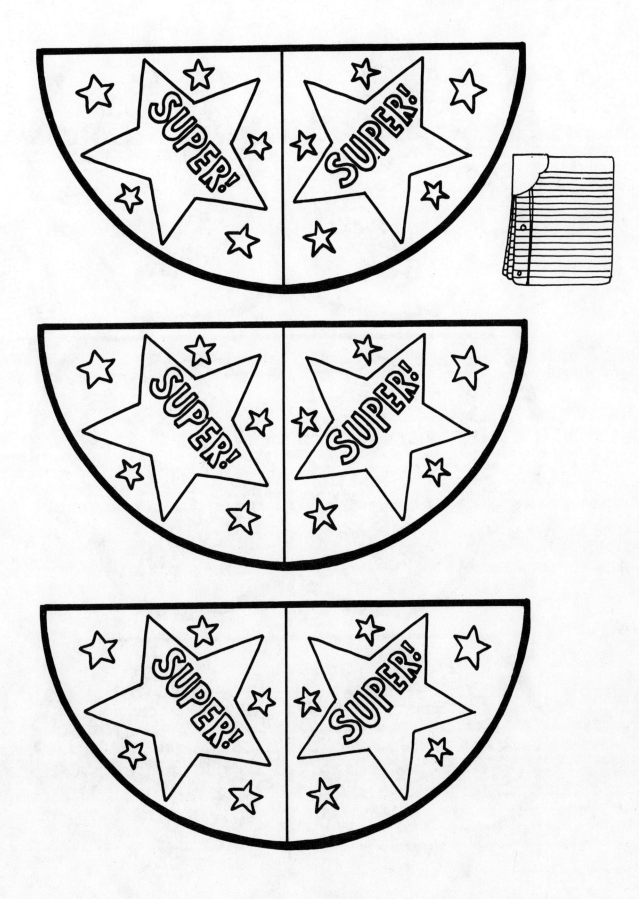

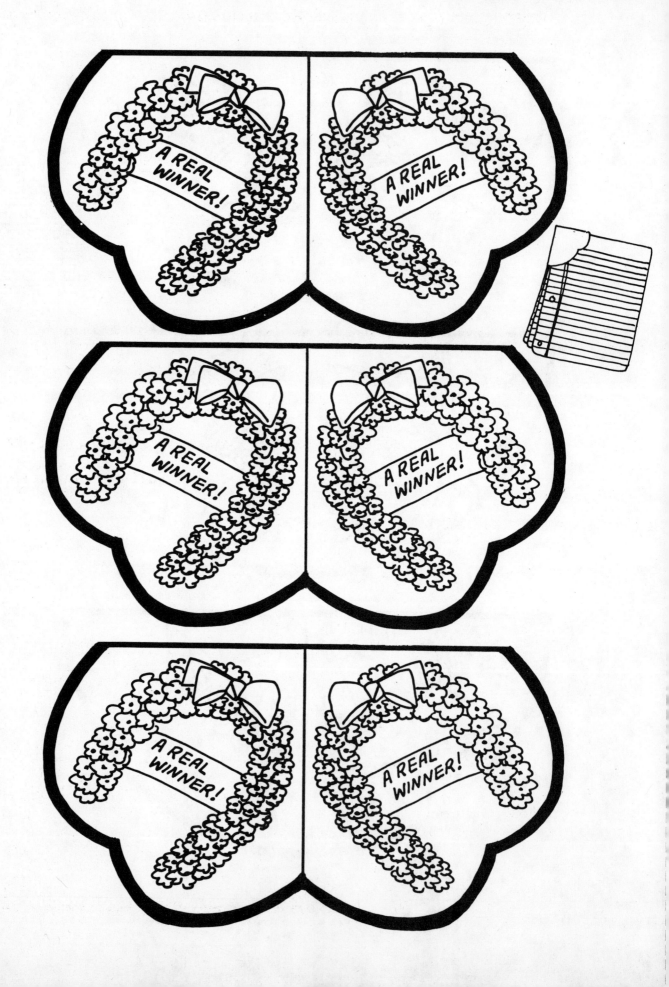

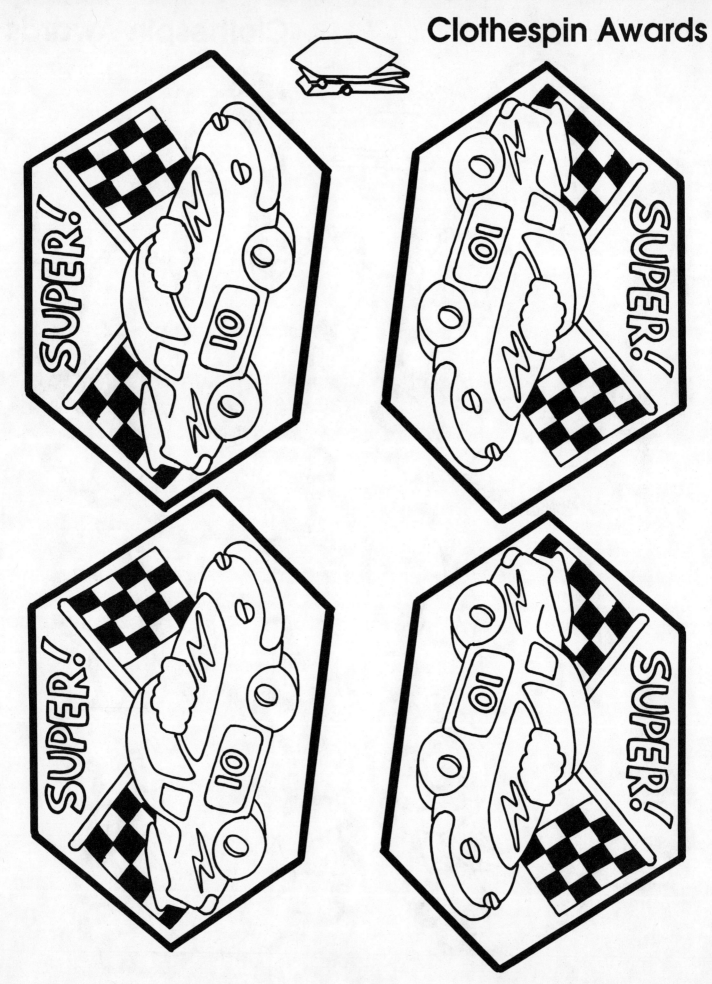

This award is given to

Student's Name

for

Signed

Date

Hall
of
Fame
Award

This award is given to

_____

Student's Name

for _____

Date _____   Signed_____

Let's Give
a Round of Applause!

Student's Name

for

Signed

Date

THREE CHEERS FOR

Student's Name

for

Signed

Date

The Champion's Court

This certifies that

_____
Student's Name

is an official

member of the Champion's Court

because of his/her outstanding achievement in

_____

_____

Signed _____

Date _____

What A Team!

Push pin

Chris Chris

STAR LINE UP

Pushpin

Laura

The "IN" Crowd

Pushpin

Stephanie

Happy Birthday Badge

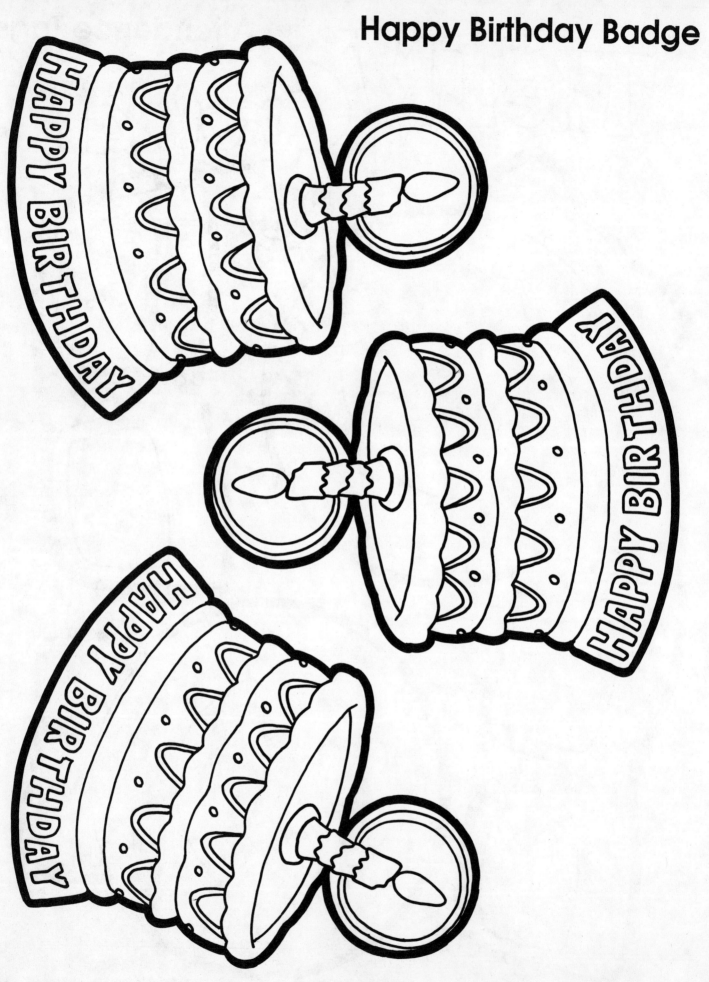

We're So Glad That You Were Born!
HAPPY BIRTHDAY!

_____
Student's Name

We're So Glad That You Were Born!
HAPPY BIRTHDAY!

_____

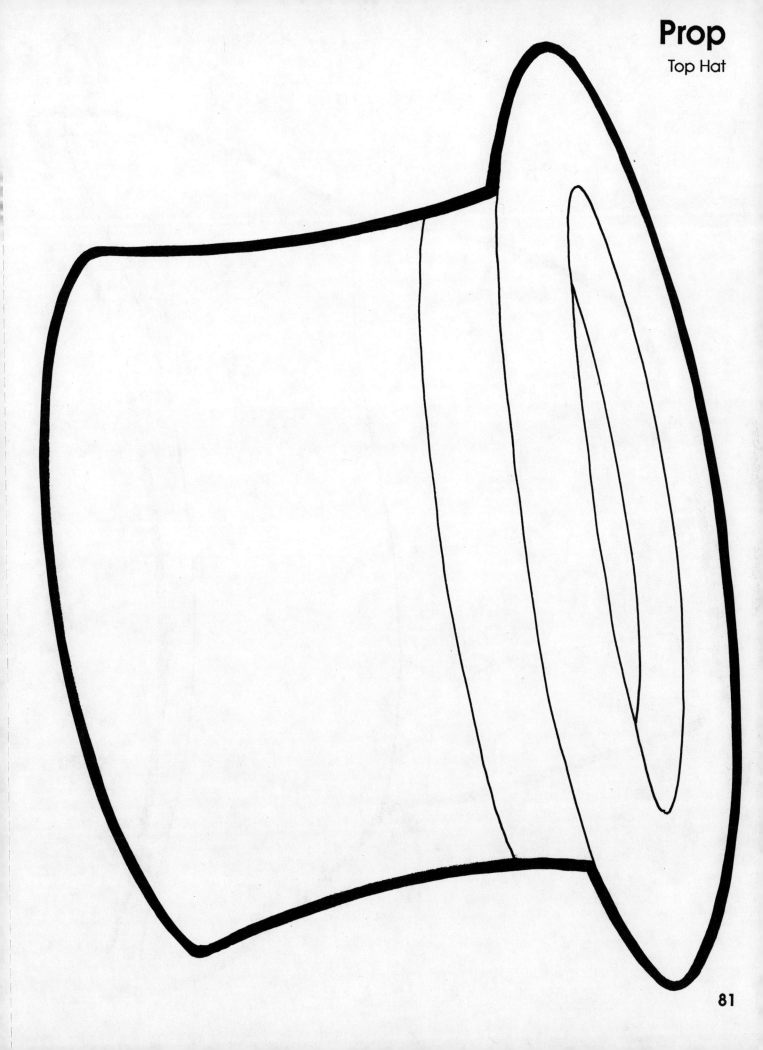

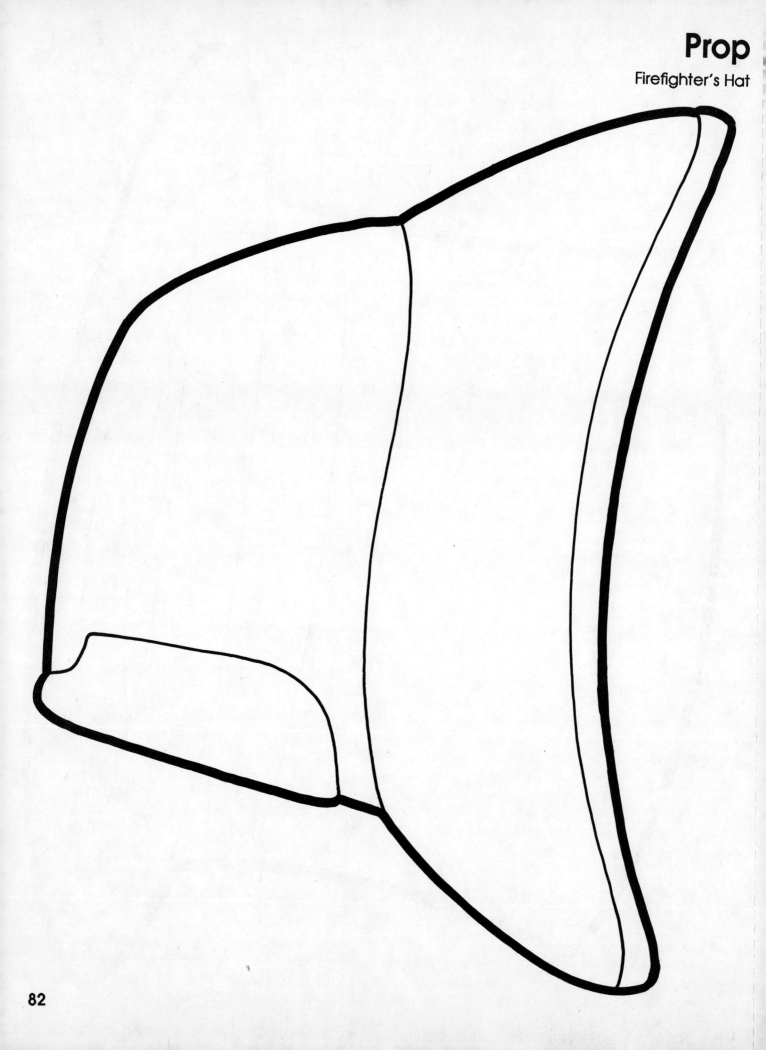

82

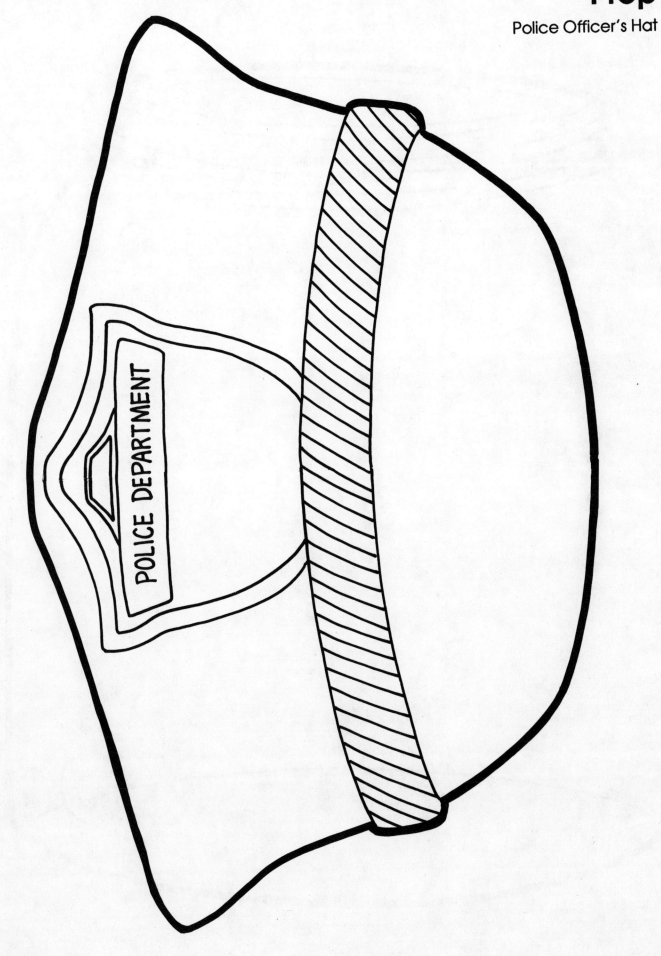

POLICE DEPARTMENT

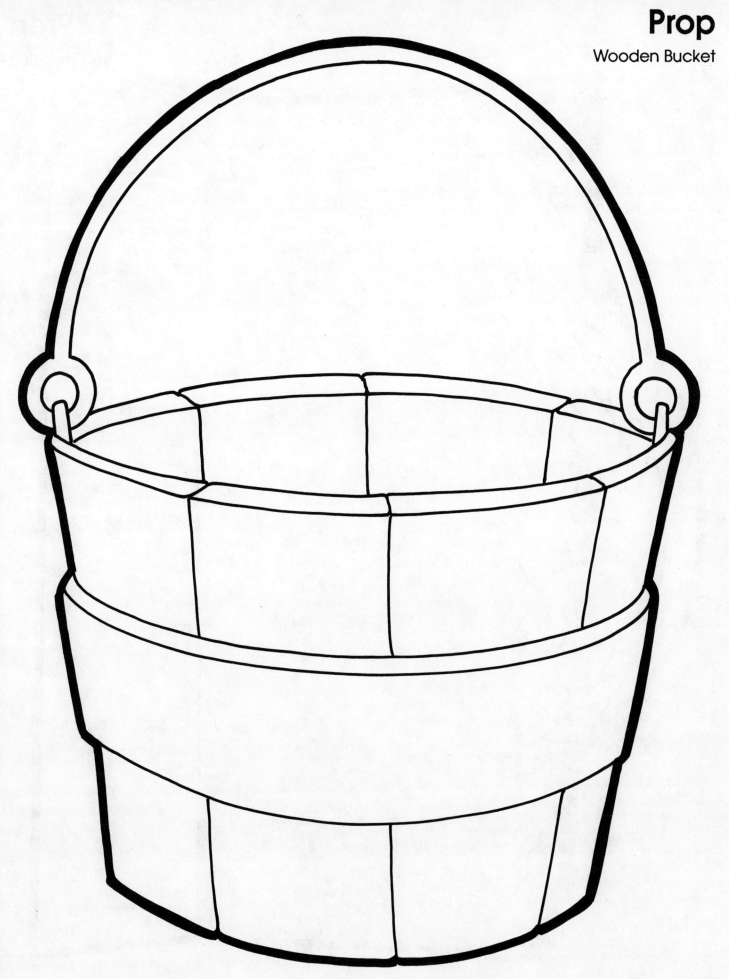

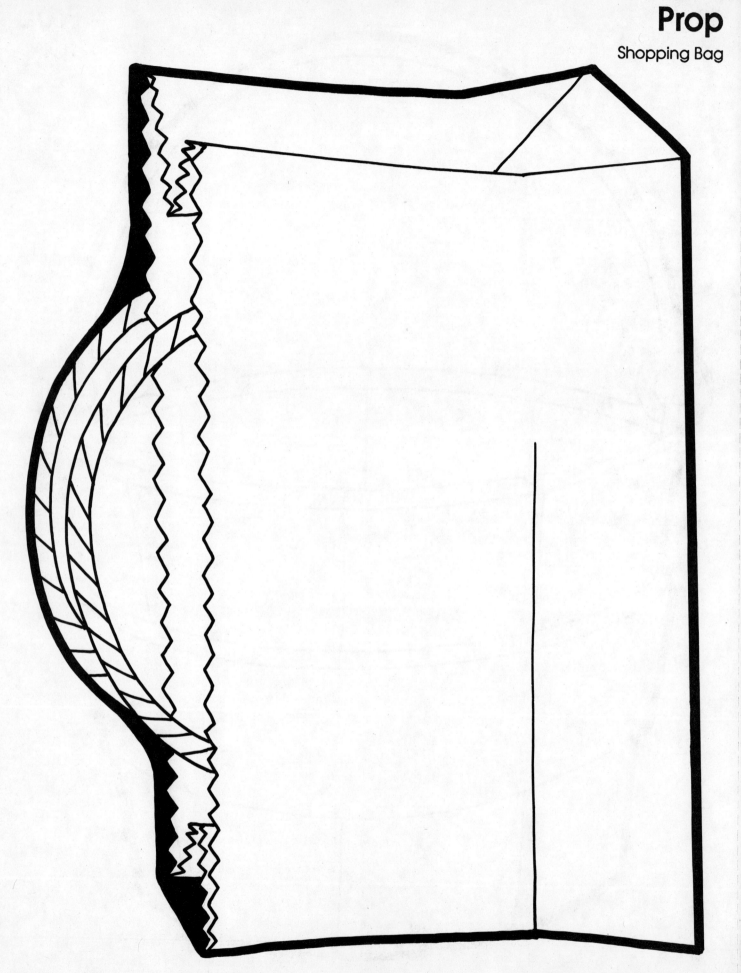

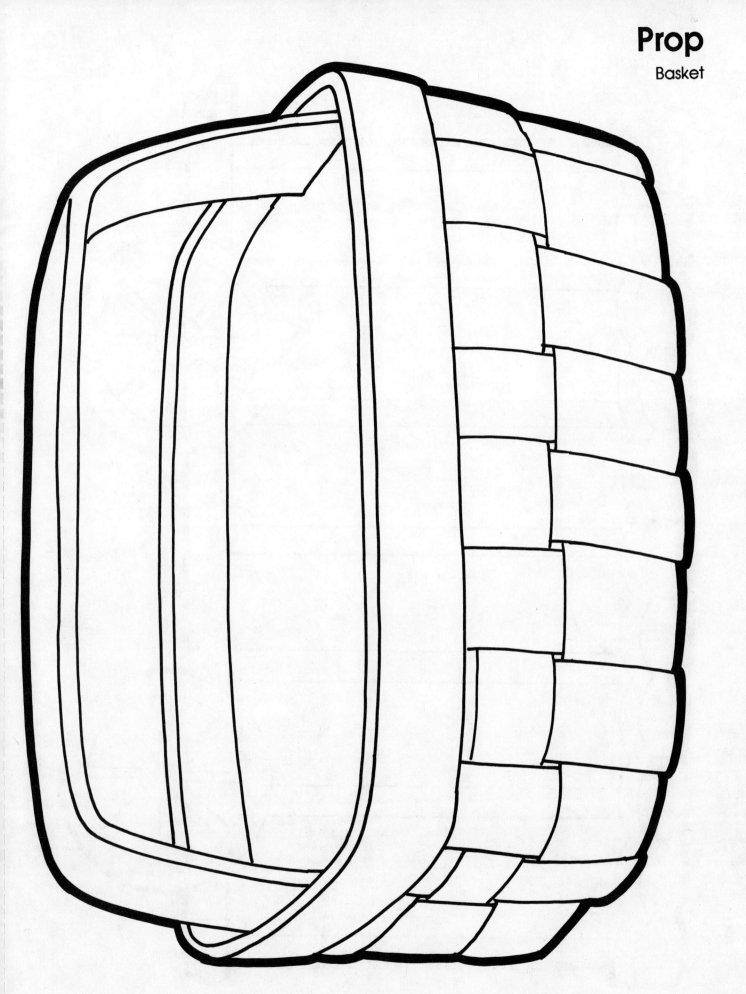

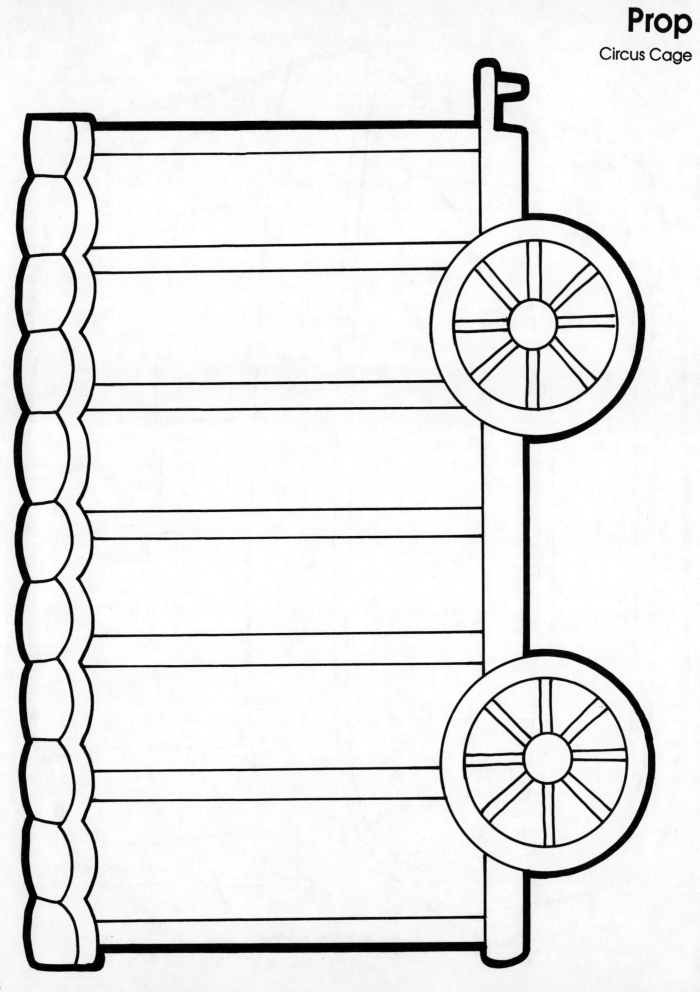

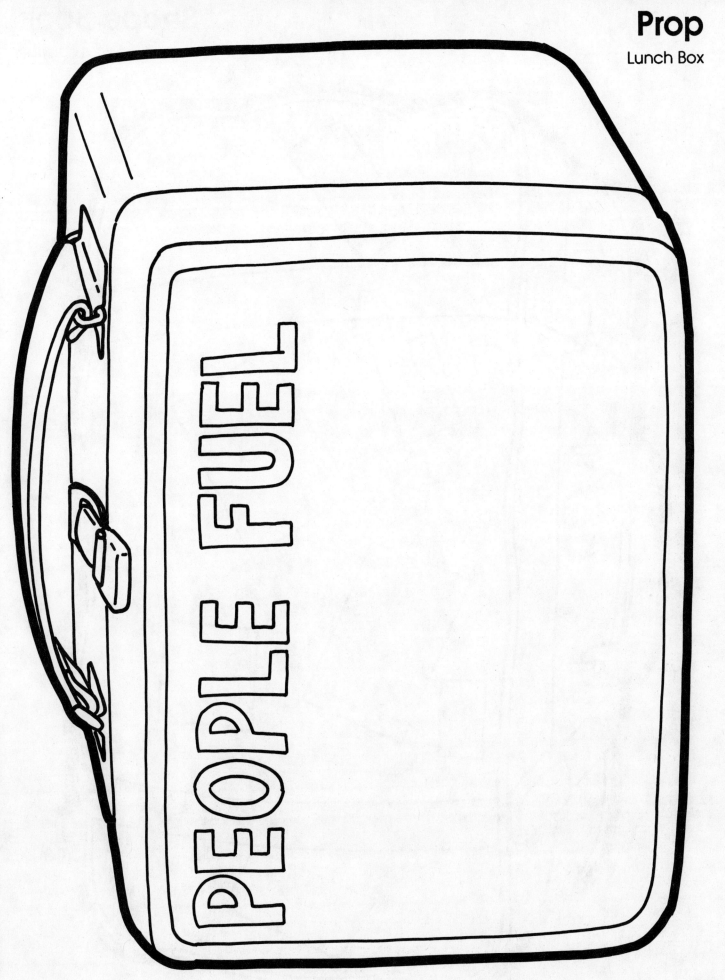

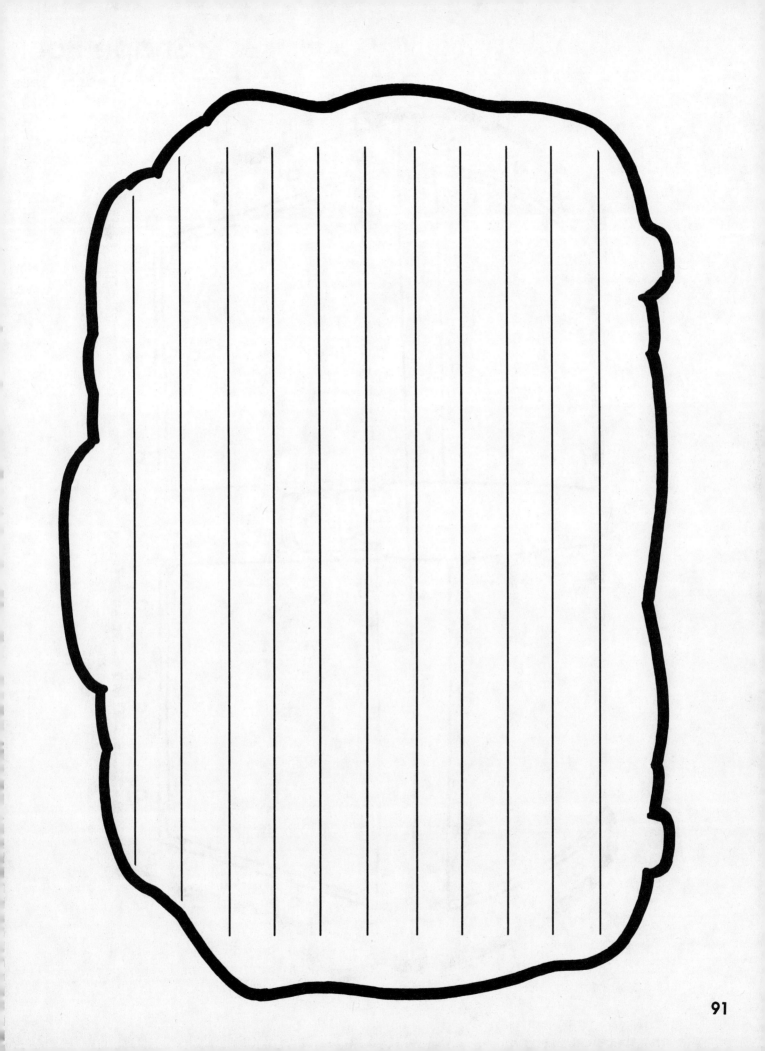

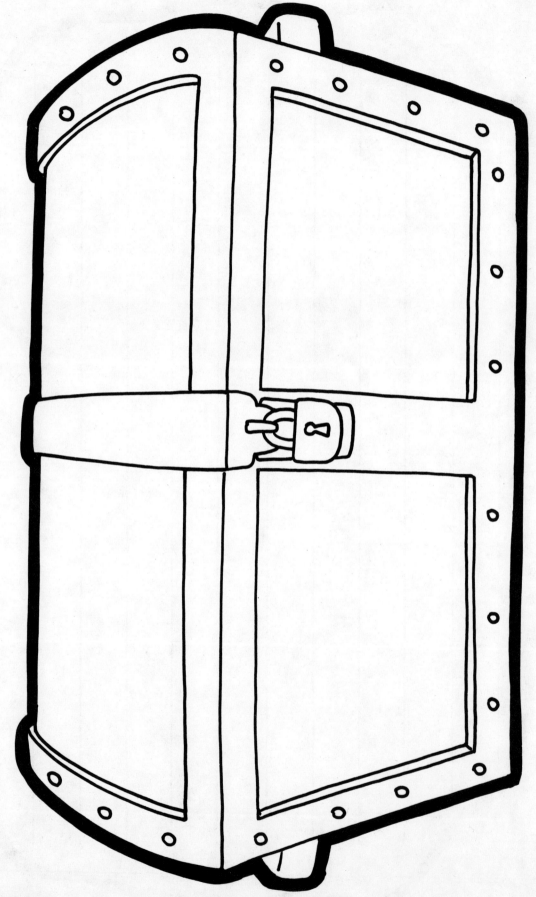

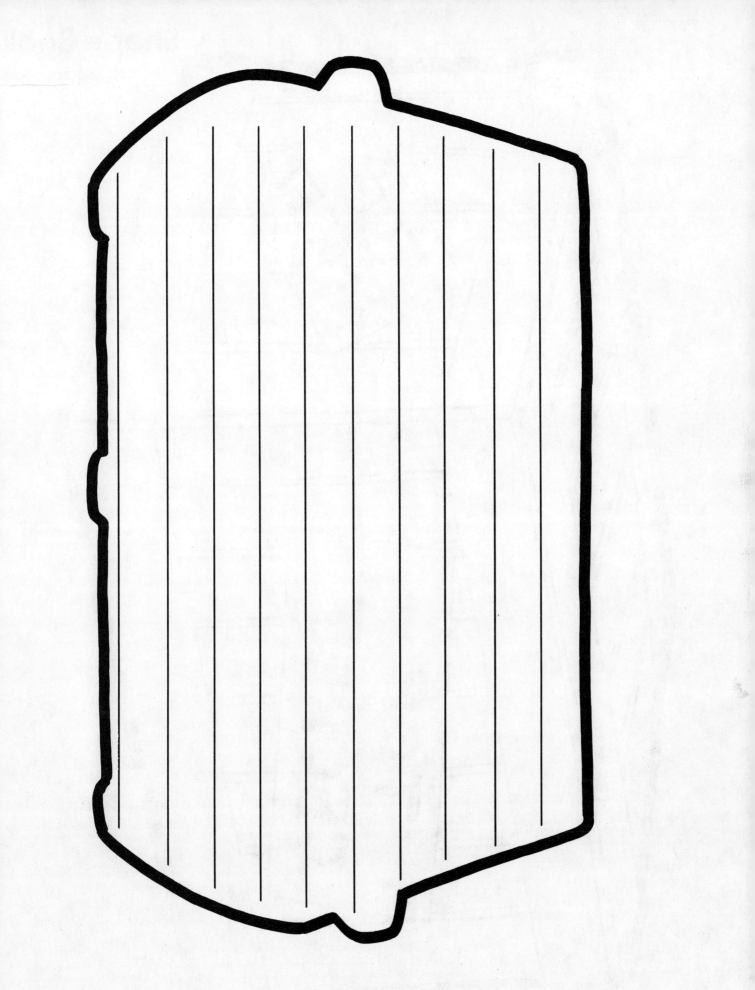

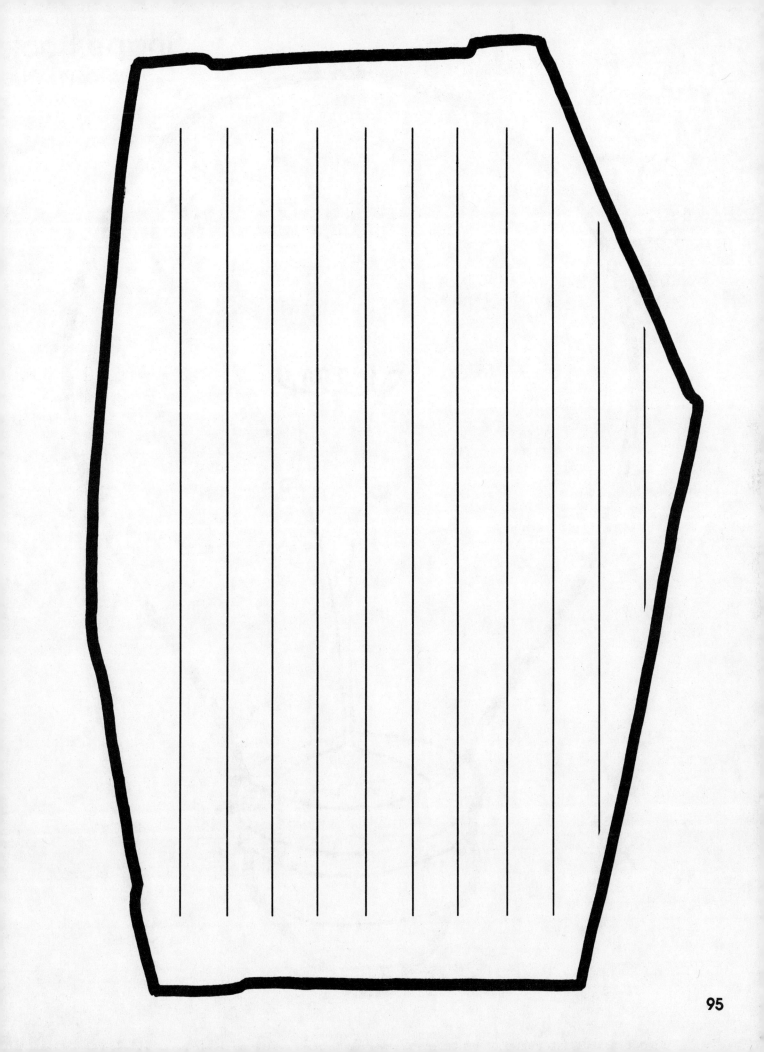

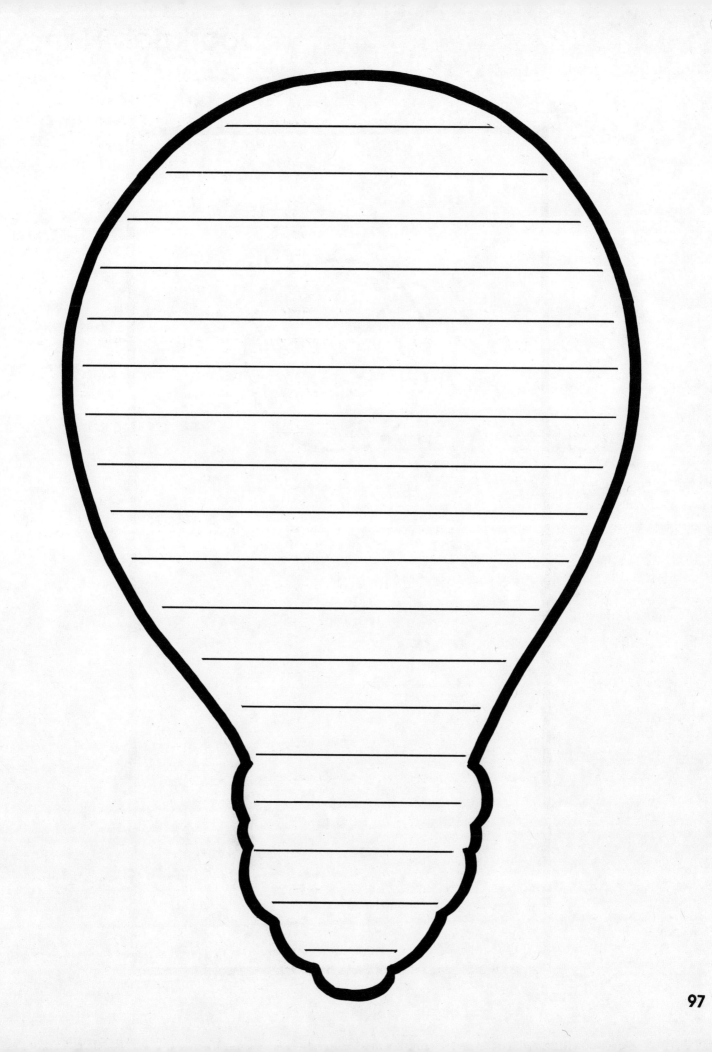

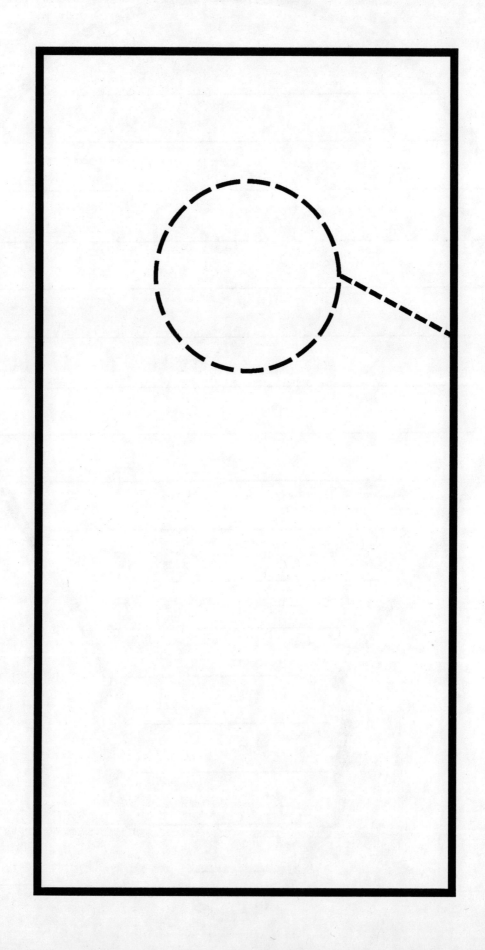

Doorknob Hanger

Inserts

On A Field Trip	Taking A Test
At The Library	In The Gym
At Recess	Out To Lunch

"KEEP ON TRYING"

A Courtly Gesture

You Did It !

MOVING RIGHT ALONG

OHAILO

It's A Party!

It's a Masterpiece!

GLUE POT

PAINT

PAINT

GLUE

SCHOOL

WELCOME BACK

MASON JAR

HARVEST TIME

Happy Holidays

BE MINE

110

Hoppin' Good Job!

April Showers
Bring Beautiful
Flowers

Follow The Wind

Dad

Smooth Sailing!

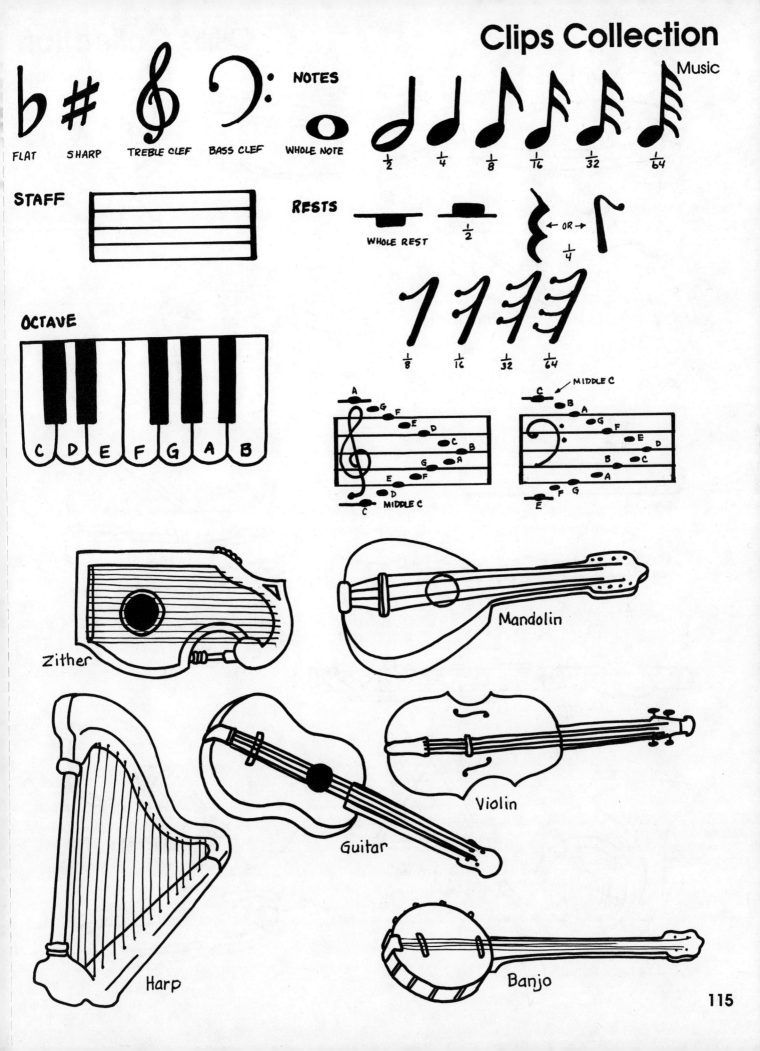

115

Clips Collection

Music

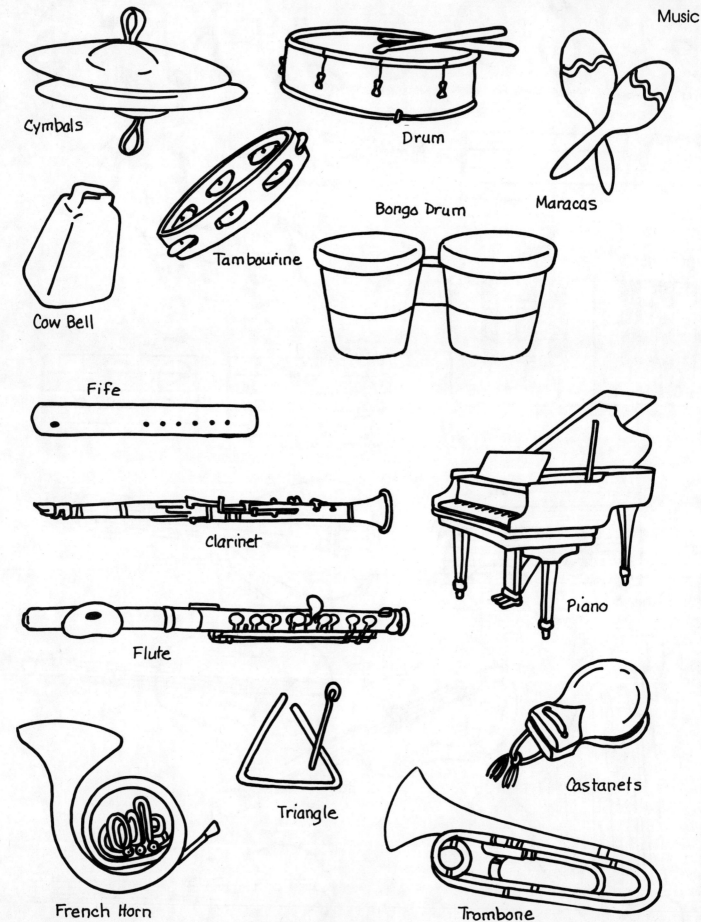

Cymbals

Drum

Maracas

Cow Bell

Tambourine

Bongo Drum

Fife

Clarinet

Flute

Piano

French Horn

Triangle

Castanets

Trombone

HAVE A CHOCOLATE CHIP BIRTHDAY

HAPPY BIRTHDAY

Happy Birthday To You!

LIBRARY

ON
OFF

Time Out

Social Studies

HEADLINE NEWS

WELCOME BACK TO

Media Center

Principal's Office

Science

FIRE ALARM

Language Arts

Fire Drill

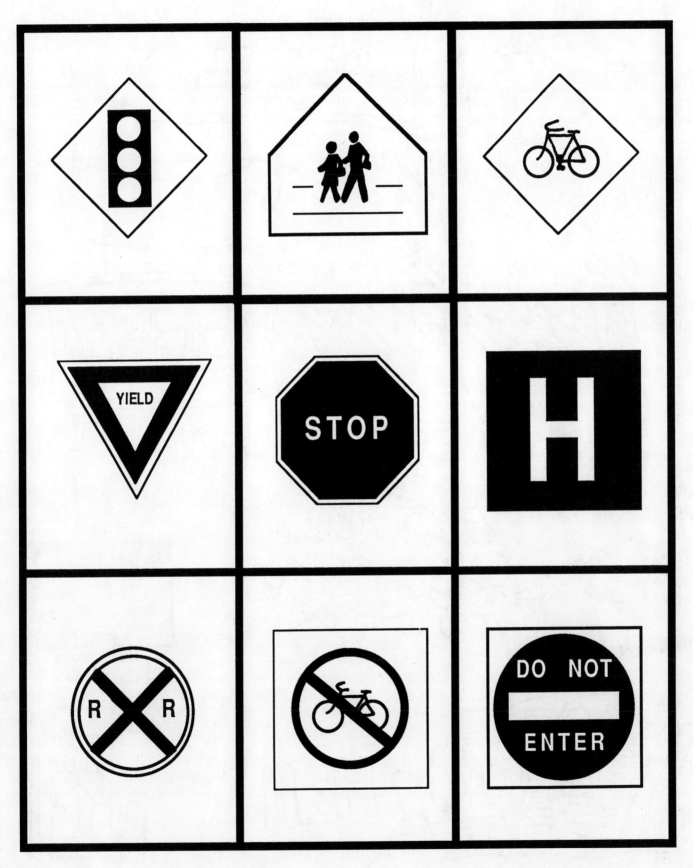

SCHOOL

Field Day

Cafeteria

P.T.A.

Spring Fall
Festival

Study Hall

EXIT

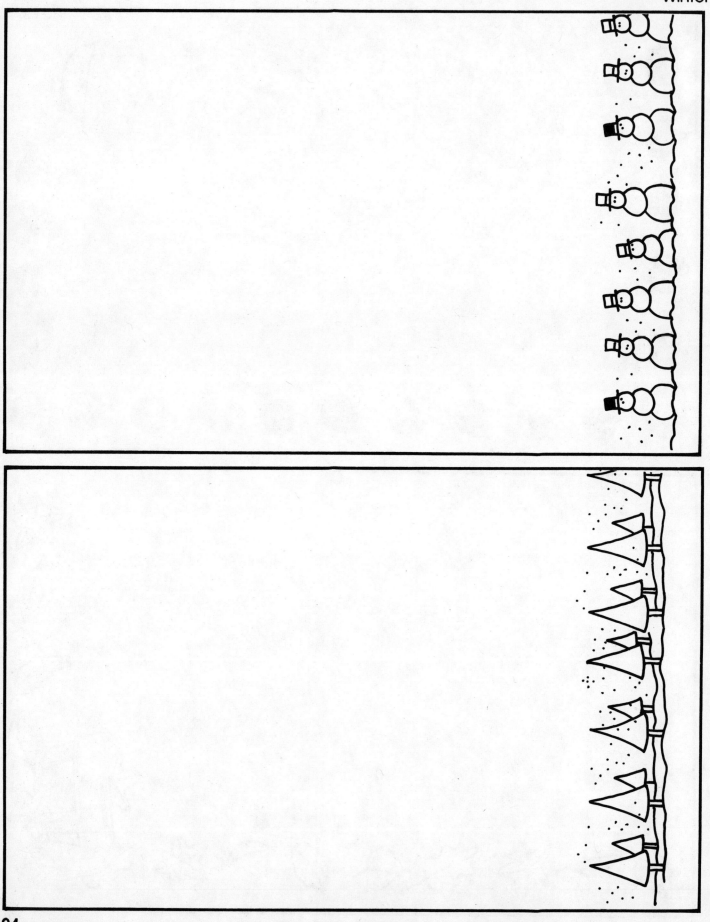

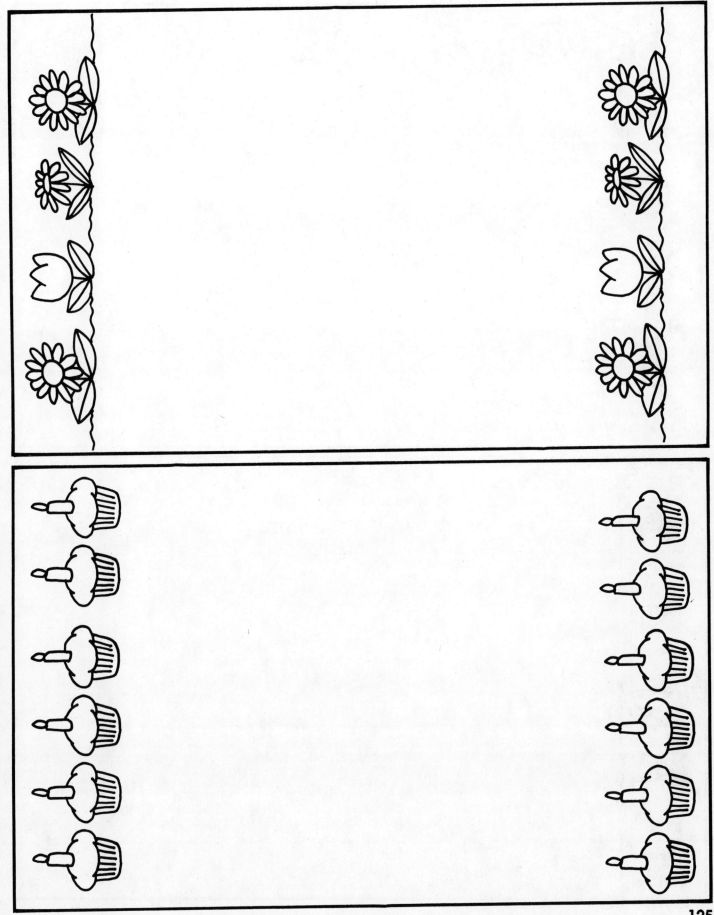

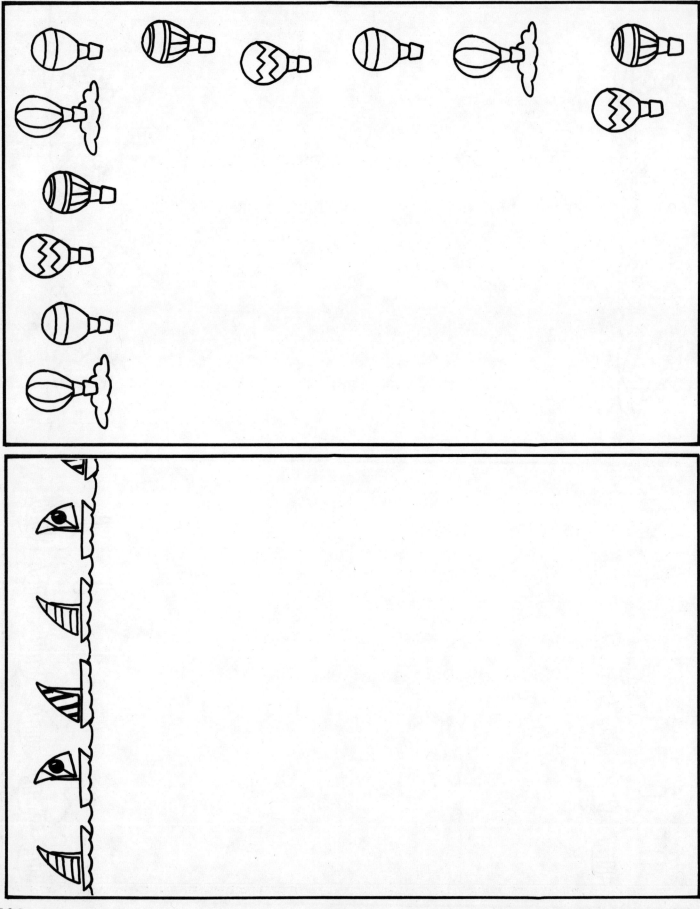

From:
The Teacher's Desk

Dear _____

_____

_____

_____

_____

_____

_____

_____

_____

_____

_____

_____

_____

_____

Free Time

_____
Student's Name

Redeem this card for
10 minutes of free time in class.

Teacher _____
Not redeemable during tests.

Extra Credit

_____
Student's Name

Redeem this card for
extra credit.

Teacher _____
Not redeemable for homework assignments.

Free Pencil

_____
Student's Name

Redeem this card for
one free pencil.

Teacher _____

No Homework

_____
Student's Name

Redeem this card for
one incomplete homework assignment.

Teacher _____
Not redeemable for book reports.

Citizen of The Week

_____
Student's Name

Teacher _____
This card entitles the bearer to special privileges for one week.

King for a Day

_____
Student's Name

Teacher _____
This card entitles the bearer to special privileges for one week.

Queen for a Day

_____
Student's Name

Teacher _____
This card entitles the bearer to special privileges for one week.

Team Captain

_____
Student's Name

Teacher _____
This card certifies that the bearer has been chosen
as team captain for the period of one week.